SEA TURTLE

ANDERS HANSON

Consulting Editor, Diane Craig, M.A./Reading Specialist

A Division of ABDO

ABDO
Publishing Company

visit us at www.abdopublishing.com

Published by ABDO Publishing Company, a division of ABDO, P.O. Box 398166, Minneapolis, Minnesota 55439. Copyright © 2014 by Abdo Consulting Group, Inc. International copyrights reserved in all countries. No part of this book may be reproduced in any form without written permission from the publisher. SandCastle™ is a trademark and logo of ABDO Publishing Company.

Printed in the United States of America, North Mankato, Minnesota
102013
012014

 PRINTED ON RECYCLED PAPER

Editor: Liz Salzmann
Content Developer: Nancy Tuminelly
Cover and Interior Design and Production: Anders Hanson, Mighty Media, Inc.
Photo Credits: Shutterstock, Thinkstock

Library of Congress Cataloging-in-Publication Data
Hanson, Anders, 1980- author.
   Sea turtle / Anders Hanson ; consulting editor, Diane Craig, M.A., reading specialist.
      pages cm. -- (Giant animals)
   Audience: 4 to 9.
   ISBN 978-1-62403-061-1
1. Sea turtles--Juvenile literature. I. Craig, Diane, editor. II. Title.
   QL666.C536H36 2014
   597.92'8--dc23
                                2013023942

SandCastle™ Level: Transitional

SandCastle™ books are created by a team of professional educators, reading specialists, and content developers around five essential components—phonemic awareness, phonics, vocabulary, text comprehension, and fluency—to assist young readers as they develop reading skills and strategies and increase their general knowledge. All books are written, reviewed, and leveled for guided reading, early reading intervention, and Accelerated Reader® programs for use in shared, guided, and independent reading and writing activities to support a balanced approach to literacy instruction. The SandCastle™ series has four levels that correspond to early literacy development. The levels are provided to help teachers and parents select appropriate books for young readers.

Emerging Readers   Beginning Readers   Transitional Readers   Fluent Readers
(no flags)   (1 flag)   (2 flags)   (3 flags)

contents

HELLO,
SEA TURTLE!

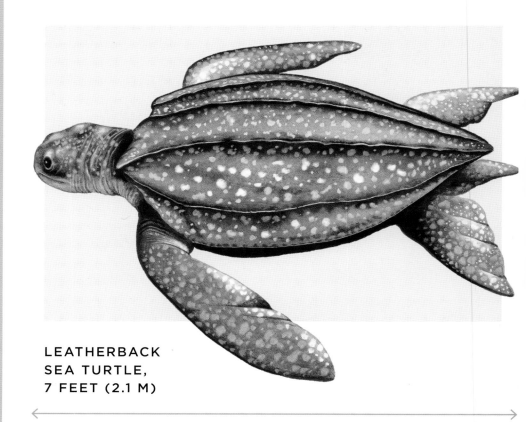

LEATHERBACK
SEA TURTLE,
7 FEET (2.1 M)

HUMAN,
6 FEET
(1.8 M)

Sea turtles are large **reptiles**. They live in water.

There are seven types of sea turtles. The leatherback sea turtle is the largest.

WHAT ARE YOU UP TO?

Sea turtles spend most of their time underwater. But sea turtles have to breathe air. So they often stick their heads out.

NICE FLIPPERS!

Sea turtles have **flippers**. Their flippers help them swim. Sea turtles also use their flippers to move on land.

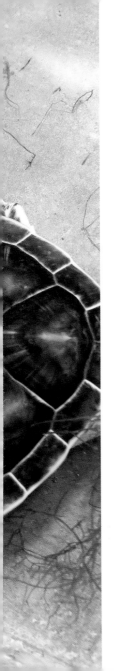

COOL SHELL!

Most sea turtles have hard shells. But the leatherback doesn't. Its shell is leathery.

Leatherback sea turtle

WHERE DO YOU LIVE?

Sea turtles live in oceans. They are found all over the world.

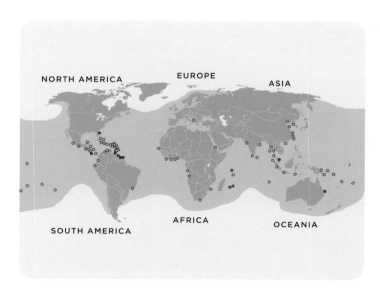

WHAT DO YOU EAT?

Sea turtles eat sea plants and animals. They eat fish, clams, and seaweed.

DO YOU HAVE A FAMILY?

Female sea turtles lay their eggs on beaches. They cover the eggs with sand. When the babies **hatch**, they crawl to the ocean. Adult sea turtles live alone.

WHERE ARE YOU GOING?

Female sea turtles return to the beaches where they were born. They lay their eggs there. **Male** sea turtles never leave the ocean.

ARE YOU IN DANGER?

Most sea turtles are **endangered**. Boat **propellers** sometimes hurt sea turtles. Sea turtles can also get caught in fishing nets.

QUICK QUIZ

Check your answers below!

1. **The leatherback is the smallest sea turtle.** TRUE OR FALSE?

2. **Sea turtles use their flippers to move on land.** TRUE OR FALSE?

3. **All sea turtles have hard shells.** TRUE OR FALSE?

4. **Sea turtles live all over the world.** TRUE OR FALSE?

1) False 2) True 3) False 4) True

GLOSSARY

endangered – close to extinction.

female – being of the sex that can produce eggs or give birth. Mothers are female.

flipper – a wide, flat limb of a sea creature, such as a manatee or a turtle, that is used for swimming.

hatch – to break out of an egg.

male – being of the sex that can father offspring. Fathers are male.

propeller – a device with blades used to move a vehicle such as an airplane or a boat.

reptile – a cold-blooded animal, such as a snake, turtle, or alligator, that moves on its belly or on very short limbs.